Copyright © 2025 Catch a Leaf Publishing

All rights reserved. This book or any portion thereof may not be reproduced or used in any manner whatsoever without the express written permission of the publisher, except in the case of brief quotations embodied in a review and certain other non-commercial uses permitted by copyright law.

9781068612275 Ducks Paperback
9781068612282 Ducks Hardback

Text and Illustrations by Siski Kalla
Design Audrey Sauble
Published by Catch a Leaf Publishing

**Also available in the series:
Let's Explore Snails, Let's Explore Moths**

JNF037020 JUVENILE NONFICTION / Science & Nature / Environmental Conservation & Protection
NAT045000 NATURE / Ecosystems & Habitats / General
JNF003170 JUVENILE NONFICTION / Animals / Pets
JNF051000 JUVENILE NONFICTION / Science & Nature / General

First Edition, 2025

To all the children growing up in towns and cities who love nature.

To all the children who'll move a snail off the path, scoop a ladybird out of water, and gently capture a moth to release it outside.

To all the children who care about wildlife – you are amazing!

Let's explore ducks!

Can you answer this question for me?
What makes a duck a duck?

Can you identify all the birds? It's useful to be able to ID birds, including ducks, by their silhouettes as that's often all you'll see!

A duck has wings and feathers!

But so do other birds... so what makes a duck a duck?

Answers, left-hand page, from top: rose-ringed parakeets, great spotted woodpecker, bluetits, robin, cormorant, pochard duck, tufted duck; right-hand page, from top: blackbird, magpie, mallards, mute swan and shoveler duck.

All birds have wings and feathers. But a duck's feathers are special. They are waterproof!

Rain? Like water off a duck's back!

When a duck dives underwater, the fluffy 'down' (shorter softer feathers) stays completely dry. How? Oil! Ducks use their beaks to spread a waxy oil over their feathers. This oil repels water. It stops the water from making the feathers wet.

See how the feathers are layered? That helps keep the water off too.

Try this experiment!

Fill a shallow white dish with baby oil or sunflower oil. Mix a small amount of water with 2 different food colourings. Drip a little of one colour into the dish. See how it separates (it doesn't mix) from the oil? That's the oil repelling the water. Now add a drop of the other colour – it will mix with the coloured water, but not the oil!

What else makes a duck a duck? Ducks swim! Can all ducks swim?

Some ducks just stick their heads underwater to eat and these are called dabblers; other ducks dive right under and swim! They are called diving ducks.

A duck's feet don't have feathers.

Their feet are smooth to help them move better in water.

Can you think of anything humans use to swim better? Yes, fins! (Also called flippers.) They are very similar to a duck's webbed feet.

Duck feet have bones in them that help keep the shape of the foot so it creates resistance (push) against the water, so they can move forward. Fins have 'ribs' in them made of harder plastic which do the same thing.

Why do ducks swim? To eat!

Ducks eat grass, aquatic (underwater) plants, insects, seeds, fruit, fish, and small crustaceans. As they eat plants *and* animals, they are called omnivores.

Are you an omnivore? Or a herbivore?

A duck can also fly. Can all ducks fly?

Most ducks can fly. But not all! Some species of steamer duck cannot fly. And domestic ducks can't usually fly either. (Domestic ducks are not wild but have been tamed and bred by humans over many, many years, changing the way they look and behave.)

So flying isn't necessarily what makes a duck a duck. Geese can also fly. So what makes a duck different to a goose?

Clear the landing! Duck incoming!

Unlike us, birds have hollow bones*. Why hollow? Bones with nothing inside make flying easier as a bird is much lighter than other animals whose bones make them too heavy to fly.

*Unless you're a penguin, ostrich, or other flightless bird! They don't have hollow bones.

Ducks are smaller than geese, but bigger than coots...

But you can guess whether a bird is a duck or a goose by looking at its neck, too. If its neck is short, it's probably a duck. If it's longer than 10cm it's probably a goose. If the neck is really long and thin, it's probably a swan! (And, in general, geese are almost always bigger than ducks.)

I'm a rail. That's a type of water bird. Call me coot. Or coot-y, if you like!

People thought I was cute, they brought me to the UK from China!

Goosander

Shoveler

Common eider

What else makes a duck a duck? A beak!

This is one of the things that makes a duck a bird. All birds have feathers and a beak.

A duck uses its beak to feel and find food. And if you watch a duck eat you'll see it doesn't chew, like we do!

Ever get that feeling you're being watched?

Squid, octopus, and cuttlefish also have beaks – but they're definitely not birds!

What other animals have beaks?

Platypus (Australia)

I've got a beak, webbed feet, and I lay eggs... but I'm not a bird. I'm a mammal!

A duck has a hard 'nail' at the front of its beak for foraging, often a different colour to the rest of the beak. See if you can get close enough to a duck to check!

I've got fur and I produce milk — although I 'sweat' it out instead of producing it via my teats like most mammals.

Terrapin, invasive species in the UK

Platypuses are weird!

Have you looked in the mirror lately? You've got a green head!

Some ducks have bristles along the inside edges of their beaks, called lamellae, to help them filter their food. Other ducks have serrated edges (like a saw) to help them hold wriggly fish.

Ducks can see behind them!

Ducks have good eyesight! They can see nearly all the way round their heads without moving, because their eyes are on the sides rather than facing forward.

Ducks have three eyelids! An upper and lower eyelid, like you, and a third see-through eyelid that protects their eyes while flying or swimming.

"I'm a platypus and lay eggs too!"

A female duck lays more eggs when there's more daylight. She'll sit on the nest almost all the time, only leaving for an hour or so in the morning and afternoon to feed.

Ducks and birds aren't the only animals to lay eggs, though! Insects, amphibians, reptiles and the platypus all lay eggs.

"I lay eggs that are tiny compared to these!"

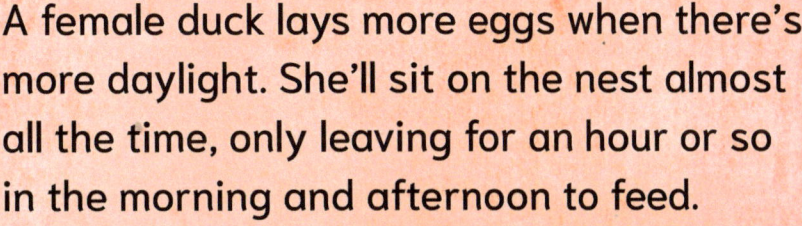

"I lay my eggs in the sand."

Ducklings can swim as soon as they crack out of their egg. They can feed themselves, too. They stick together for about ten days to avoid being attacked by predators.

What does a duck eat and what eats a duck?

Predators of ducks include dogs and foxes, and cats. Magpies, herons, crows, rats and even squirrels will eat duck eggs and even eat a duckling if they get the chance.

Grey heron

Don't even think about it!

I'm related to 'sea monkeys', aka brine shrimp!

Ducks quack!

Not all ducks quack, but there aren't any other animals that quack, so quacking is unique to ducks. Unique means being the only one of that kind. Like you! You are also unique!

What do you call a duck that steals? A robber duck!

Did you know that ducks in cities are louder than ducks in the countryside? Research by English language professor Dr Victoria De Rijke found that ducks in East London had louder and different quacking sounds from those living in Cornwall, where the quacks were 'longer and more relaxed'.

"The ducks are taking over! Waddle we do?"

A duck also waddles. Can you waddle like a duck?

Ducks move more easily in water than on land. Their 'bottoms' swing from side to side as they waddle. Like mine!

Ducks prefer to be around other ducks. They're sociable. A group of ducks can be called a paddling, a waddling, a flock, or a raft. Do you prefer to be around ducks? Or humans? Or both?

Why do we need ducks?

Ducks are important food for lots of other animals!

Predators – animals that hunt and eat other animals – of ducks include foxes, weasels and also birds. Birds such as herons, crows and magpies will take a small duckling if they can, and they love eggs too. Terrapins, which are found in UK waterways (though they're not native), will also eat a duckling!

A kite (secondary consumer) is easy to recognise even when it's just a silhouette, because of the forked tail.

Ducks can be primary consumers (only eat plants), or secondary consumers (eat plants and animals). Tertiary consumers eat animals that eat other animals. What kind of consumer are you?

I'm a tertiary consumer and an omnivore! I eat meat, I eat animals that eat other animals (tuna, for example), as well as plants (broccoli is my favourite).

I'm a secondary consumer — I'm an omnivore but I only eat animals that eat plants. I love beef best!

I'm vegan, I only eat plant foods. That makes me a primary consumer!

Sssh, don't tell the others that I'm a tertiary consumer!

We are all primary consumers, we eat plants.

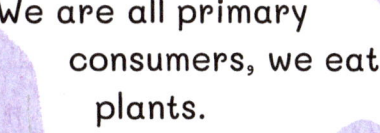

Do ducks need our help? Yes, they do!

Duck habitats – ponds, rivers, canals, lakes – are in trouble. Rubbish in our waterways can injure them, it damages plantlife, makes the water polluted and looks horrible, too!

Ducks get injured by rubbish, as well as discarded fishing lines and hooks.

How to DO something

Team up!

Get your classmates involved in a clean up.

Organise a street or local park litter collection.

Or sign up to a citizen science project (see the last page of the book for more on this).

Reuse and recycle to avoid adding more rubbish to our waterways. Reusable metal bottles are a good alternative to plastic bottles. Refillable cleaning bottles made of glass are better than plastic too.

Just as important: buy used products or find out if they are sustainably produced. A single new cotton T-shirt, for example, might use 1727 litres (650 gallons) of water to produce!

Ask your parents if you can rewild parts of your garden if you have one. Allowing native plants to grow will help retain moisture, provide food and shelter for wildlife, and use less water. Let's go WILD!

Feed the ducks!

Keep your dog on a lead near waterways, to protect the ducks.

Ducks need healthy food like frozen peas, oats, sliced grapes, chopped lettuce. Bread causes problems because they get full without getting the nutrients they need. Ducks also enjoy mealworms which you can buy at your nearest pet shop.

Nutrients are substances that help your body survive and grow.

Shoveler duck

Ducks are all over the world!

There are only around 160 species of ducks in the world. In towns in the UK, you're most likely to see the ducks shown on these pages.

Watch out for males and females of each species! They often look very different.

Mallard duck

I'm having an identity crisis. Am I a duck or a goose?

You're a duck! You're part of the shelduck family!

Why did the hoomans call me a goose then? Who's a silly goose now?!

Egyptian goose

Goosander

Goldeneye

Some ducks you might see aren't native to the UK. These include the pretty mandarin ducks (from China), and also the Egyptian goose, which is actually considered a duck.

Mandarin duck

My ancestors are from China. People from the UK took some of them and kept them in collections, but then they escaped... and now I live in the UK!

Duck craft!

Choose a duck species you'd like to make or make up your own. It's easy and you can use your hand as a template!

Art recipe ingredients

thick paper (coloured or colour it yourself exactly as you like)

scissors

glue

1) Draw around your hand on the paper, make sure your thumb is pointing up!

2) Cut out around the lines on the paper as shown.

Earthwatch Europe

Every purchase of this book is a positive change for our planet. For every sale of this book 50p goes to support Earthwatch Europe, an environmental charity with science at its heart.

Earthwatch works to create a world where we live in balance with nature by helping people to protect the nature around them. Earthwatch builds meaningful nature connections and gives people the tools they need to fight for our planet. Working alongside communities and organisations, Earthwatch builds an understanding and a love of nature, and helps everyone to protect the natural world. Guided by science and powered by people, Earthwatch creates change through connection.

Find out more at Earthwatch.org.uk

Some other great organisations

The Wildlife Trusts
There are 46 Wildlife Trusts in the UK, go to www.wildlifetrusts.org to find one local to you.

RSPB
The RSPB is a charity for the conservation of birds and nature. The website www.rspb.org.uk is useful for IDing birds, too, with photos and information.

The Swan Sanctuary (London).
A charity dedicated to the treatment of swans and waterfowl, based in Shepperton, UK. www.theswansanctuary.org.uk

For more information about books in the Urban Wildlife Explorer series and to learn more about our urban wildlife, head to www.urbanwildlifeexplorers.com

Look out for these! They're hiding in this book!

I'm Siski, the author and illustrator of this book – and I love visiting ducks at the park! These photos are of 'Miles', a duck we found in our local park. He* had been abandoned there in the middle of winter. He was very tame and seemed very hungry! Domestic ducks usually eat grass and food given by humans. But Miles couldn't reach the grass because there were lots of dogs around scaring him back to the water. With some help from a man who was also worried, we took him home to keep him safe. We gave him peas (which he loved!) and water, and called a local wildlife rescue centre. They were wonderful and came to get him, releasing him on their property on a large lake with the other ducks and birds.

*We didn't know if Miles was male or female! But we chose his name because the man who helped us was called Miles, so we named him the same! Read about other wildlife adventures we've had at www.urbanwildlifeexplorers.com

Webbed feet answers: Top paw = beaver; top right = frog; bottom right = Newfoundland dog; bottom left = mallard duck.

www.ingramcontent.com/pod-product-compliance
Lightning Source LLC
Chambersburg PA
CBHW041543040426

42446CB00003B/220